# MEKONG

# MEKONG

A Journey on the Mother of Waters

MICHAEL YAMASHITA

Takarajima Books

*For Lil, my editor and best friend*

MEKONG: A JOURNEY ON THE MOTHER OF WATERS
COPYRIGHT © 1995 BY TAKARAJIMA BOOKS, INC.
PHOTOGRAPHS AND TEXT COPYRIGHT © 1995 BY MICHAEL YAMASHITA.
PHOTOGRAPHS ON PAGES 6-7, 8-9, 14-15, 35, 62-63, 64-65, 80, 81, 82-83, 108-109, 116-117,
122-123, 126-127, 128-129: COPYRIGHT © 1993 NATIONAL GEOGRAPHIC SOCIETY
INTRODUCTION COPYRIGHT © 1995 BY STANLEY KARNOW.

TAKARAJIMA BOOKS
200 VARICK STREET, NEW YORK, NY 10014
TEL: 212-675-1944, FAX: 212-255-5731

BOOK AND COVER DESIGN: BILL MARR
TEXT EDITORS: ELIZABETH BIBB AND SUSAN BELL
MAP: DAVID GRIFFIN

THE STAFF AT TAKARAJIMA BOOKS FOR MEKONG IS:
AKIHIKO MIYANAGA, PUBLISHER
KIYOTAKA YAGUCHI, ASSISTANT PUBLISHER

ISBN 1-883489-09-01
LIBRARY OF CONGRESS CATALOG CARD NUMBER 94-060219

PRINTED AND BOUND BY C&C OFFSET PRINTING CO. LTD., HONG KONG

QINGHAI

Zadoi

TIBET

SICHUAN

BORDER CLAIMED BY CHINA

INDIA

CHINA

Dali ● Erhai Lake

YUNNAN

MYANMAR

Jinghong ●

VIETNAM

LAOS

HANOI ★

Golden
Triangle

Luang Prabang ●

Nam Ngum

VIENTIANE ★

YANGON ★

THAILAND

BANGKOK ★

Angkor Wat ●

Khone
Falls

CAMBODIA

Tonle Sap

PHNOM
PENH ★

Ho Chi Minh
City ●

Cantho ●

Phung
Hiep ●

North

0
100 Kilometers

100 Miles

# CONTENTS

PHNOM PENH

CAMBODIA

*Sisters at play splash in the*
*murky waters of the Mekong*
*as it churns through Phnom*
*Penh, the largest city located*
*on the river, with a*
*population of one million.*

VIENTIANE • LAOS

*A woman practices the ancient art of dip-net fishing in the shallow water along the banks of Vientiane, Laos's sleepy capital city.*

*preceding pages:*  PHUNG HIEP • VIETNAM

*A pentagram of canals in the Mekong Delta converge at the floating market along the banks at Phung Hiep.*

*Over 1,800 miles of canals sprawl throughout the fertile delta, the most densely populated provinces in Vietnam.*

# INTRODUCTION

*by Stanley Karnow*

*Stanley Karnow, a former correspondent in Southeast Asia, won the Pulitzer Prize in history in 1990 for his book* In Our Image: America's Empire in the Philippines. *His other books include* Vietnam: A History.

OF ALL THE RIVERS I KNOW, FROM THE MAJESTIC NILE AND MIGHTY MISSISSIPPI TO THE BUSY THAMES AND PLACID Seine, none enthralls me more than the Mekong. Nourished by the eternal snows of Tibet, the roof of the earth, it twists and turns for nearly three thousand miles—tumbling down the rugged mountains of southwestern China, cutting through the jungles of Laos, after marking its border with Myanmar, bending to delineate the boundary with Thailand, traversing Cambodia and finally fanning out across the delta in Vietnam before splaying into the South China Sea. Inextricably intertwined with the vast area's mythology, history, economy, politics and culture, the Mekong is the vital artery that pumps life into the different peoples touched by its banks.

The river's diversity is reflected in assorted names. In Tibet it is called the Dza Chu (Water of Stone), in Cambodia the Tonle Thom (Great Water), and in Vietnam the Cuu Long (Nine Dragons). The word Mekong is derived from Mae Nam Khong, a Thai/Lao term roughly meaning Mother of Waters.

No photographer portrays this fascinating panorama as vividly as does Michael Yamashita. Trekking from its lonely source to its multiple mouths, he spent months capturing its brilliance, its variety and, above all, its humanity. All that is missing from his pictures are the sounds and smells of the river.

I FIRST ENCOUNTERED THE MEKONG IN THE LATE 1950s, when as a reporter I began to cover Southeast Asia. France had recently been defeated in its attempt to retain its colonial hold over Vietnam, Cambodia and Laos, collectively called Indochina, and the crueler American war had not yet erupted. In the quiet interlude I could roam the region in relative security, savoring its marvels and mysteries.

My earliest journey was to Laos, the landlocked little kingdom of valley peasants and a mosaic of hill tribes whom anthropologists identified by the different colors of their dress. Vientiane, the administrative seat, was a sleepy riverside town that primarily stirred for holidays. From there I drove to Luang Prabang, the royal capital and a crucible of Buddhism. At dawn, monks in saffron robes would shuffle in single file through its dusty streets, holding out their brass begging bowls to be filled with food by the faithful, who thus earned merit for their own afterlife.

The main crop of Laos at the time was opium, cultivated chiefly on the slopes above the Mekong by the Hmong, one of the country's minorities. I traced them as they extracted the gummy juice of poppies, and shaped it into loaves that porters carried on their backs to river towns like Houei Sai, where Laos, Burma and Thailand meet. There dealers operating with official connivance shipped it to Bangkok and Hong Kong to be refined into morphine and heroin, and thence to Europe and America. Despite international efforts to stop it, the warlords who dominate the drug traffic in the so-called Golden Triangle have since introduced such modern methods as refining the opium on the spot, and the business is bigger than ever.

The Mekong flows gently between Laos and Thailand before entering Cambodia not far from the Tonle Sap, the large lake near the magnificent temple complex of Angkor, one of the world's wonders. Its construction was started in the ninth century and continued for 500 years. Not only were its builders master architects, but engineers of the period used the river to create a sophisticated system of canals and irrigation ditches that bequeathed Angkor a food surplus. The Cambodian chief of state, Prince Norodom Sihanouk, who cherished his nation, would stage elaborate festivals at Angkor to evoke its former grandeur. The one I attended in 1967 for President Charles de Gaulle of France featured dancers and elephants, and remains engraved in my memory. The war in Cambodia and natural erosion of its stone have endangered the stone temples of Angkor, and unless urgent conservationist steps are taken, their future may be in doubt.

As the war in Vietnam gained momentum, the Mekong delta became a battlefield between the South Vietnamese forces and the Vietcong guerrillas. At first, river life was deceptively calm. Villages seemed serene as farmers transplanted rice and small boys splashed in the flooded fields. By chance I was near the delta on July 8, 1959, when the first two American soldiers were killed, and I revisited the zone repeatedly during the years that followed. The fighting soon escalated and the delta has still not recovered from bombings and shell fire; its water tables were disrupted by bomb craters, and its trees blighted by shell fragments.

Legend has it that the lands of the Mekong were founded by a Hindu traveler and his wife, the daughter of a *naga*, or serpent king. Combining the cultures of India and China, the basin later became the cradle of powerful, competitive civilizations. Before it crumbled in the sixteenth century, the Cambodian empire reached into Burma, Thailand, Laos and Vietnam. Burma at one time ruled over much of Thailand, and Vietnam conquered Champa, a land only remembered today for its bronze sculpture. The states of the region largely owe their present configuration to the European imperialists who arrived during the nineteenth century, mainly in quest of commerce.

Foremost among them were the French, who believed that the Mekong would serve as a trade route to south China. In 1866, they mounted an expedition that met with disaster when they discovered that the river was not navigable. Nevertheless, they carved out a colonial dominion in Indochina that lasted until 1954, when they were crushed at the famous battle of Dien Bien Phu by the Communist-led Vietminh nationalists. But they still dream of restoring their cultural influence in the region, as reflected in the 1993 visit to Vietnam by French President François Mitterrand, the first Western leader to go there since the war with the United States ended eighteen years earlier.

Though experts have maintained that the Mekong has enormous economic potential, plans for its development have been delayed by the Vietnam war and the Khmer Rouge genocide in Cambodia. But the return of peace to the region has raised hopes that the river can be harnessed to improve crops and generate electricity. The Mekong may well change—and, in the process, lose some of its pristine charm. If so, Michael Yamashita's already valuable photographs will be an even more precious record of the way it was.

TIBETAN PLATEAU

QINGHAI, CHINA

*The place the Tibetans call the
sacred source of the Mekong is a
frozen river bed at an altitude of
17,000 feet on the Tibetan
Plateau. In search of a campsite,
our guide Meiga crosses the three
feet of ice under which the
westernmost headwaters of the
Mekong trickle:*

ERHAI LAKE

YUNNAN CHINA

*Cormorant fishermen on*
*Erhai Lake, which forms*
*an important part of the*
*Mekong's watershed,*
*train their birds to*
*retrieve their catch.*

*Barrage nets strung across
the Tonle Sap Lake, the
great regulator of the
Mekong's waters, trap a
bounty of up to 50 tons of
fish per day. Fishermen
smack the water with sticks
to drive fish toward the
back of the net.*

19

YUNNAN • CHINA

*The Mekong has chiseled gorges as deep as 9,900 feet in Lamaden, in northern Yunnan.*

*Herders returning home cross a narrow rope suspension bridge strung across a ravine.*

DZA CHU

# Water of Stone

MY JOURNEY BEGAN AT THE BEGINNING, 17,000 FEET HIGH on the Tibetan Plateau in China's Qinghai province. Here the snow-fed headwaters of the Mekong are given the first of its local names—in Tibetan, *Dza Chu* (Water of Stone), because of its origins in the bare rock pinnacles of the Plateau.

I was to reach the Mekong's icy source and from there follow the river, the world's twelfth longest, on its 2,600-mile run south to its mouth in the warm waters of the South China Sea, off Vietnam. My research on the river had turned up precious little on the upper reaches of the Mekong. The most up-to-date descriptions I could find were from a 1926 expedition led by the legendary *National Geographic* explorer, Joseph Rock, but the Rock expedition had only visited the northern section of Yunnan province over 400 miles to the south. As far as I could

tell, no Western journalist had ever been to the source, let alone photographed it.

Here was the dream assignment, the opportunity of a lifetime: to do a story that had never been done before for the great photography magazine, *National Geographic*. My traveling partner and good friend, writer Tom O'Neill , and I arrived in China well-prepared for the challenge.

First there were the inoculations. Aside from the usual tetanus, gamma globulin, cholera and yellow fever vaccines, there were shots for Japanese encephalitis, polio and bubonic plague. I thought these were wiped out years ago, but apparently not, at least not where I was going.

Then there was the bulky *Geographic*-issue medical kit—the descriptions and dosage instructions for its contents covered four pages. Pepto Bismol, Lomotil, Doxycycline and Dialyte for dysentery and diarrhea; Bactrim for "fevers of undetermined origin"; Larium for malaria prophylaxis; Fansidar for malaria treatment; Sodium Sulamyd ophthalmic solution for eye infections; Percocet, Advil and aspirin for general pain; Diamox for altitude sickness; industrial-strength insect repellent and sunscreen, Neosporin, Valisone, water purifiers, first aid and snake-bite kits rounded out the list. What could possibly harm us with this medicine chest in our packs?

Nonetheless, the trip started with a headache, a high-altitude one that took hold as we flew into Lanzhou, the airport nearest our destination. Already at 5,000 feet, we squeezed ourselves and eight cases of camera and camping gear into two battered Chinese Jeeps and set off into the starkly beautiful, dust-colored landscape. The Tibetan Plateau lay 1,000 miles to the west, uphill all the way. Our primary concern was to avoid altitude sickness. Our solution was to spend the next week traveling, fifteen hours a day over brutally rough roads, stopping only to refuel, thus daily adapting to the rarefied atmosphere.

As it turned out, my headache lasted the entire month, brought on only partly by the thin air. After less than two days on the road, we ran into the first of what were to be many problems. Our two white-gloved, chain-smoking Han Chinese drivers assigned to us by the government refused to take us any higher unless we paid more money. The burden fell on Wen Dong, our guide from the Chinese Journalists Association in Beijing, to negotiate. In China, negotiations are invariably long and always complicated. And Wen Dong, we were to discover, was a skillful practitioner of the art.

A wiry five-feet four-inches and 130 pounds of pure verbal tenacity, he relished figuring out how to beat the system.

He had visited no less than nineteen different government departments and agencies to secure the necessary permissions to get us this far. But even with his two-inch sheaf of official papers, we always seemed to be one short of satisfying the greedy local officials we encountered. Their sole job, it seemed to us, was to impede our progress. This first negotiation with the drivers went our way. With the proper "fees" paid to the officials, after three cups of tea (we began rating the complexity of a negotiation according to how many cups of the ubiquitous green liquid we consumed before reaching a conclusion), we were allowed to fire our recalcitrant Chinese drivers and hire two Tibetans to take us the rest of the way.

The contrast in driving styles between Chinese and Tibetan was immediately striking. The Chinese seemed as jumpy as the battered Jeeps they were driving. The Tibetans, on the other hand, drove those same vehicles with joyous, reckless abandon. They swigged beer and played Hong Kong disco tapes at top volume and scattered paper prayer messages out the window as we sped by sacred sites along the road. We stopped often to treat overheated engines (because the boiling point of water is much lower at high altitudes, it was necessary to constantly replenish the water in our Jeeps' radiators). Then there were the numerous delays getting stuck in frozen streams and on muddy roads.

But the troubles posed by nature were only minor irritations compared to our dreaded dealings with officialdom. Our every move was monitored through government inspections and checkpoints. There were endless negotiations for gasoline, for permission to take a picture, permission to stop overnight in a town, even for permission to move on the next day. And always there loomed the threat that the entire trip might be canceled by some zealous bureaucrat who had no idea why we were there in the first place.

We finally arrived in Zadoi, two Jeeps and six officials heavier. We needed extra guards (for which we paid, of course) to protect us from wolves, we were told. At this point, deep in southern Qinghai, just a few days away from our goal, the stress of all the bitter negotiations took its toll on Wen Dong. After a two-day, umpteen-cup negotiation for guides and six horses to take us to the Mekong's source, Wen Dong came down with acute altitude sickness. We sent him, with pounding heart and head, and unable to walk, to a hospital at a lower elevation, armed with a bottle of oxygen and our Diamox pills.

But even without Wen Dong as an interpreter, we had no trouble communicating with Meiga, the big, smiling Tibetan herder in charge of our horsepack trip to the source. We found his campsite where the road ended on a frozen mountain stream. I pitched my two-man canary-yellow dome next to his black yak-hair tent. Meiga, with the curiosity of a child, marveled at my tent's light weight and strength, running his fingers over the nylon fabric and mosquito netting. He also insisted on exploring the entire contents of my camera bag, settling on the 16 mm full-frame fisheye and the 600 mm telephoto as his favorite lenses. We were then invited to his tent for some Tibetan-style hospitality.

Sitting on yak wool blankets, we ate slabs of dried yak meat, washed down with yak-butter tea, and warmed ourselves over the yak-dung fire. So vital is the animal to the economy here that the nomad's name for yak is *nam*, which also means *wealth*. It didn't take much to figure out that Meiga's herd of a hundred yaks must make him a wealthy man in this part of the world. He and his wife, three children, father and brother-in-

law were completely self-sufficient thanks to this versatile beast of burden.

At dawn we saddled up for the final stretch. We learned that there are actually two sources of the river: One, high up on a glacier where our Chinese guards had refused us permission to go, and a second, the spiritual source, according to Tibetan legend, located behind a holy mountain where Tibetans go to worship the god who brings water for their animals. Meiga told us, "We believe that if you drink the source water, you will live a long life. And if the animals drink it, they can grow very fast and have no diseases. This river is the blood that runs into our bodies."

That day, we followed Meiga through blinding snow and equally blinding sun, over a vast, treeless sea of grass. I tried focusing on the immensity of the place by photographing the tiny silhouette of a wild donkey or the occasional nomad far off in the distance against the stark, barren, undulating hills. Meiga looked oddly majestic atop his sturdy white Mongolian pony, decked out in a black turban, with a pearl-handled dagger jutting from his waistband and black high-top basketball sneakers completing the picture. As I was admiring his fashion sense, he suddenly reached into his saddlebag, pulled out a handful of colored prayer papers printed with Buddhist scripture and threw them high into the wind. We had arrived!

We had made it to the source of the Mekong. The holy mountain Meiga had told us about, a solitary, breast-shaped, 200-foot-high hill, barely hid the hourglass-shaped stream, frozen under three feet of ice, that ran behind it. As we rode to the edge of the ice, the sound of trickling water grew louder. Tom and I, Chinese guards and Tibetan guides, horses and dogs, all knelt by the stream and drank to our long lives.

TIBETAN PLATEAU

QINGHAI · CHINA

*Beyond these mountains*
*of the towering Tibetan*
*plateau lies the sacred source*
*of the Mekong at an*
*altitude of 17,490 feet.*

*Our guide, Meiga, and his
family spend the summer
at this encampment near the
sacred source of the Mekong.
A yak-skin tent houses Meiga,
his wife, Daji, his brother-
in-law, Bachairen, and
their six children.*

TIBETAN PLATEAU · QINGHAI · CHINA

*With a hundred yaks, Meiga's family is considered prosperous in a culture that counts wealth by the size of a man's herd.*

*As impervious to the bitter cold as her ice-encrusted yaks, Daji begins her daily milking chores.*

29

TIBETAN PLATEAU • QINGHAI • CHINA

*The yak is central to the livelihood of the Tibetan herders, providing milk for yak-butter tea, meat, dung for cooking fires, and skins for clothing and tents.*

QINGHAI

CHINA

*Our first sight of the
Mekong as more than
a frozen stream came
outside Zadoi, the
northernmost town on
the river. The water's
graceful bend belies the
wild, uncontrollable
rapids nearby.*

31

ZADOI · QINGHAI · CHINA

*Despite a climate so brutally harsh that washing becomes a rare event, daily life goes on. Children attend*

*classes at this one-room schoolhouse in Zadoi between chores with their families' herds.*

ZADOI • QINGHAI • CHINA

*Yak herders drive their animals through treacherous narrow mountain passes on the outskirts of Zadoi.*

LANPING • YUNNAN • CHINA

*With the closest bridge 25 miles away, villagers of the Lisu tribe still use this ancient and precarious form*

*of river crossing to reach the far banks of the Mekong.*

LANPING · YUNNAN · CHINA

*The inhospitable gorges carved by the Mekong near Lanping, in northern Yunnan, keep the river unused and unnavigable*

*until its final 90-mile stretch through China, as it spills into Laos.*

ZHOUCHANG • YUNNAN • CHINA

*Her wares on her back, a vendor—of the Bai tribe—takes her vegetables to Zhouchang Market on the shores of Erhai Lake.*

# Turbulent River

THE MOST STRIKING FACT ABOUT THE MEKONG IN CHINA is the extent to which it has been ignored. It was the middle of June, we had been traveling on the Mekong for more than a month, and I had yet to take my first picture of anyone actually using the river. Not a boat, a bather, not even a fisherman, only an occasional solitary figure drawing a bucket of water. A few reasons were apparent. For one, Tibetans only bathe once a year, usually in spring, due to the harshness of the climate. But more to the point, the current runs so fast and furious that people are afraid of it and keep their distance from it. Raging white water, whirlpools and rapids have made it impossible to navigate all but the last hundred of the thousand miles of the river that flow through China. For these reasons, the Chinese have aptly named it *Lancang Jiang* (Turbulent River).

As for the lack of fishermen, a Lamaist monk in Zadoi explained it this way: "There are many fish in the river, but Tibetans do not allow themselves to eat them. The river is used for burying accident victims and the fish help carry the dead to the afterlife. A human should make his body a gift to another living creature." Consequently, I didn't find fish on the menu until the lower reaches of Yunnan province.

In sparsely populated northern Yunnan, the Mekong drops an incredible 15,000 feet cutting enormous gorges as deep as the Grand Canyon. Without warning or explanation, the Chinese government withdrew permission to travel this stretch, one of the river's most spectacular. As I learned later a detour was ordered because they did not want journalists to see the large concentrations of army troops and police amassed in the region to prevent antigovernment demonstrations. It was the 40th anniversary of China's forceful takeover of Tibet, and the authorities, concerned over the possibility of protests, were not taking any chances.

We picked up the river again a few hundred miles downstream in Lanping, a center for mining. The river had lost none of its might, cascading through chasms as deep as 3,000 feet. In this region the most common method of crossing the river was by rope bridge—a single strand of cable strung at a steep angle over the river. Using a sling attached to a pulley wheel, the rider hooks on the cable and slides down like a high-wire stuntman suspended several hundred feet over the white water. It would be another 200 miles downstream before we were to find a bridge where our Jeeps could cross.

It is this awesome topography that has kept the Mekong in its near pristine state. But as I was to discover, its days as a wild and free river are numbered. Rounding a bend on one of the few roads that run north to south along the banks of the river, I was astonished to find a 350-foot-high wall rising out of the riverbed. Hundreds of tiny figures clambered over an intricate web of scaffolding scaling both sides of the wall. This was the Manwan hydroelectric dam, the first on the Mekong, scheduled for completion in 1995. And if the Chinese government has its way, a string of eight more dams will be built over the next 30 years, turning the "turbulent waters" into a placid 300-mile reservoir stretching from the Lao border clear into canyon country, an obedient energy source for Southeast China.

My Chinese chaperones encouraged me to take pictures for a change, obviously proud of their country's technological achievement in building this colossus in an otherwise rugged no-man's-land. It was certainly hard to imagine whom this dam might be benefiting—having passed only a few barefoot flintlock rifle– or crossbow-armed locals along the roadside.

But no sooner had I found my subject than I once again ran afoul of the guards. I had ambled over to a group of several hundred brown-clad workers wearing woven bamboo construction hats who were squatting around large baskets taking a rest. I pushed through the crowds and found those baskets filled with millions of creepy-crawling green grasshoppers, which the men were devouring by the handful. I shot two frames before my guards jumped on me, wresting the camera out of my hands. It took my guide, the diplomatic and once again healthy Wen Dong, the rest of that day and a dozen cups of tea to get me out of this would-be international crisis. Apparently the men were prisoners forced to work on the dam project. I had inadvertently ruffled official feathers by photographing them on their lunch break. After this incident, the welcome mat was pulled out from under me, and it became obvious it was time to move on.

Our subsequent views of the river were frustratingly brief and unspectacular as we headed downstream into the tropics. Roads ran east/west, the river north/south. Brief glimpses of the river were often followed by days of driving to the next road/river junction. Even though I was at wits' end with my Chinese guards following my every move, the trip had been at least bearable when I had beautiful and amazing subjects; but without anything to shoot, my anxiety began to show. Finally our luck changed rolling into Dali, on Lake Erhai, a major feeder to the Mekong. Yunnan is home to 24 of China's 55 minorities, thus having the most varied ethnic population in China. And Dali, with eleven minorities living within its water basin, must surely be its most colorful city. We identified each minority by the colors of its costumes. The Bai wore blue and pink with a red headdress; the Hovi, all black, with silver belts and jewelry; the Jinuo, yellow and red and betel nut–colored teeth; the Dai, the colors of the rainbow.

It was planting season, and the flooded rice paddies were splashed with color: yellow, orange, raspberry and blue-smocked women dotted the landscape, bent over newly transplanted green rice shoots. Starved for picture possibilities the last two weeks, I overshot, running innumerable rolls of film through my cameras. My diet, too, became much more colorful, shifting away from the bland rice gruel, steamed bread and instant noodles that I'd been used to in the north to papayas and mangoes, sticky rice and real (handmade) noodles.

Farther downstream near Jinghong, in the heart of Xishuangbanna, our final destination in China, I began to notice that here villagers, rather than fearing or ignoring the river, seemed to welcome it. The banks were lined with women and children, gleefully cooling themselves in tropical heat, washing their sarongs and shampooing their hair in what now had become thick mud-colored water. Young boys with shaved heads, freed from their studies at the local monastery, swan-dived and cannonballed into the river from a high bank. Teenaged boys rode on inner tubes in the middle of the

current, snagging pieces of driftwood, which they would later sell in the market as firewood.

These people, members of the Dai (or Tai) minority, are of the same ethnic group that inhabits Thailand, Laos and Myanmar. The Lao/Burmese border lies a scant 20 miles downstream, but these two peoples, sharing the same language, the same customs, the same ethnic heritage, live in completely different countries, under different political systems and ideologies. Seeing a hint of the exuberance of river life to come, I was more than ready to leave China for the Lao and Thai versions of life along the turbulent Mekong.

*The village of Xizhou in
China's Yunnan province,
with its distinctive Bai-style
houses built around a central
courtyard, sits at the
northern end of Erhai Lake.*

XISHUANGBANNA • YUNNAN • CHINA

*Balancing buckets of fertilizer, a woman works in the rice paddies of Xishuangbanna, home of the Dai tribe.*

JINGHONG · YUNNAN · CHINA

*A single umbrella protects a fashionable young couple during rainy season in Jinghong.*

DALTIEN

YUNNAN • CHINA

*The 100-year-old wooden*
*Double Crane Bridge crosses*
*a tributary of the Mekong*
*at Daltien.*

DALI

YUNNAN • CHINA

*Once the rice crop is planted,*
*the Bai tribe celebrates the*
*Rao Shao Lin festival in*
*Qindong Village in Dali.*
*Bai women pray for rain,*
*a good harvest, money*
*and prosperity.*

47

MENGHAN

YUNNAN • CHINA

*Boys paddle their dugout
canoe through a polluted
pocket of the generally clean
Mekong in the village
of Menghan.*

*preceding pages:*

ERHAI LAKE

YUNNAN • CHINA

*A diver silhouetted
against the sky plunges
into the lake, a popular
tourist spot.*

PAK OU • LAOS

*Mountains resembling a Sung dynasty watercolor loom above the Mekong as it flows through Pak Ou.*

# Mother of Waters

BELOW CHINA, LANCANG JIANG CHANGES ITS NAME TO THE Thai/Lao *Mae Nam Khong* (Mother of Waters), which is contracted to *Mekong*. Here the river forms the border between Laos and Myanmar (formerly Burma), passing through 160 miles of sparsely populated, mostly inaccessible jungle. In this area, around the tri-border region known as the Golden Triangle where the river intersects Thailand, the Mekong suddenly converges with the modern world. For in this deeply forested and mountainous terrain, half the world's illicit opium supply is grown, traditionally cultivated by hill tribe farmers, such as the Hmong, the Lahu and the Yao.

I hopped a ride on a Thai border police helicopter heading for the Triangle on a poppy-field destroying mission. From our vantage point less than a hundred feet off the ground, it was easy to spot the well-tended light-colored patches of poppies against the forest's sweep of deep green, even at speeds of over 100 miles per hour. We swooped down on one steep hillside, close to the Burmese border—Lahu territory. Below us I could make out dozens of soldiers in camouflage spread out in lines along the hillsides, beating down the poppies with bamboo staves.

Raids like this one are funded by the United States Drug Enforcement Agency. Some 7,400 of the estimated 9,880 acres of opium poppy fields are destroyed each year during the harvest season between October and January, I was told, in one of the most successful drug eradication programs in the world. Coupled with the United Nations–sponsored alternative crop program, which substitutes the

53

planting of poppies with other cash crops, the Thais have been rightly proud of their winning battle against the drug trade. However, isn't it odd that the two most popular alternative crops are tobacco and coffee—a swap of one addictive export for other, albeit legal, ones?

Although the "gold" in the Golden Triangle refers to the highly lucrative opium trade, today it stands for the booming tourist trade there as well. The Triangle is the Mekong's one bona fide tourist attraction, known the world over. As the manager of the Triangle's five-star resort, Hotel Baan Boran, explained it, "It's the infamy of the place. People think they are having an adventure. They come to soak in the outlaw aura." What they find instead are several blocks of souvenir stores selling opium pipes and T-shirts, and photo ops with fully costumed hill tribe kids—one picture with one kid costs about a dollar (25 *baht*). It occurred to me that in this sad state of affairs, opium is probably the Mekong river's best known symbol, along with Thailand's famous rice whiskey of the same name.

The Triangle also marks the start of the Mekong's longest year-round navigable stretch—1,000 miles, about the entire length of Laos. From the Lao side I hired a boat to carry me as far as the river would allow. Finally, no more roads to lead me away from the river, no more breakdowns, no police or government officials to impede or question our progress. Just the constant current heading south, rocks and rapids our only worries. I spent the next three weeks in a blissful state, living aboard a 5-foot-wide, 65-foot-long cargo carrier, never more than an arm's length from the water.

It was February, the middle of the dry season, blue skies and hot sun the whole way. On the right bank was Thailand, with cars and paved roads, restaurants and power lines. On the left side was Laos, where I saw only an occasional thatched roof or a solitary figure carrying water buckets along the shore, standing out against a backdrop of dense forest. Though sharing a common language and cultural roots, Laos and Thailand could be oceans, rather than only a river, apart when it comes to standards of living. Laos is one of the ten poorest countries in the world. The 1990 average per capita income was only $140. The contrast with Thailand becomes all the more vivid knowing that Issan, the province on the right bank where modern life bustles forward, is Thailand's poorest.

For land-locked Laos, the Mekong is the country's lifeline, its most important transportation link and, finally, its greatest hope, thanks to the river's potential for hydroelectric power. All of the major towns and cities in the country lie along the banks of the Mekong, including the country's current capital, Vientiane. We stopped often to photograph gold panners working the shallows, elephants dragging huge teak and rosewood logs down to the banks, farmers working the newly exposed riverbanks rich with silt growing an endless variety of green vegetables. Each day we pulled to shore and did what everyone else did—bathed in its waters, ate its fish and fell asleep to the gentle sounds of the current.

Nowhere along the river is religion more a part of daily life than in Laos's old royal capital and second largest city, Luang Prabang. Here religion starts early—by 4 a.m., two hours before sunrise, when monks awaken for an hour of meditation and housekeeping before taking to the road for "binthabat," which is to say alms collecting, or more accurately, rice collecting. Promptly at 6 a.m., the streets of the city become alive with long queues of bald-headed men in pumpkin-orange robes — the eldest first — heading for equally long lines of women on their knees, holding big bowls of sticky rice. The women scoop rice from their bowls and dish it into the monks' huge earthen bowls. This ritual continues for miles as monks from each temple crisscross each other's circuitous routes around their compounds as they gather their daily meals. The scene reminded me of Halloween's trick or treating, the monks' robes and begging bowls replacing jack-o'-lanterns and paper shopping bags.

The Mekong comes crashing out of Laos through six miles of cataracts known as Khone Falls — the barrier that dashed the hopes of the early French explorers searching for an inland trade route to China. This one geographic feature is perhaps the primary reason for the lack of development along the Mekong to this day.

Some miles up river from the falls, I heard stories of a large fish that spouted water whenever it broke the surface. I wondered if this could be the giant catfish — the *plabuck* — the world's largest freshwater fish, which grows up to ten feet in length, weighing up to a thousand pounds. Though native to the entire Mekong, I had only heard of it being caught in the town of Chiang Khong, in Thailand, far to the north, in a yearly ceremonial ritual.

I set out in a wooden dugout called a *pirogue* to find and photograph this elusive fish, now on the endangered species list. It was not long before I spotted a creature breaching like a whale and spouting water, hearing it breathe before actually catching sight of it. I grabbed my camera, catching a shot of its white dorsal fin cresting the surface of the water before it disappeared into the river's depths. I alternately chased six of these giants, each about nine feet in length, up and down a mile-long stretch of river that sat between impassable rapids. Trapped in this small lakelike enclosure, I never got closer than 150 feet to any of them and so never got a clear shot — even with a 600 mm lens on my camera.

Though it didn't take me long to realize that the fish I had been photographing were not the elusive *plabuck*, it was not until much later that I found out my Mekong monster was actually a dolphin called the *irrawaddi*, after the river in Burma in which they still thrive.

Local fishermen told me of the terrible smell of the creatures' rotting flesh when they occasionally were caught in their nets, ruining the nets and killing themselves in the struggle to break free. There once lived dozens of these hulks here, but now only six are believed to remain. The rest were wiped out by hungry soldiers, mostly Khmer Rouge whose fishing technique employed not nets but live hand grenades tossed into a likely fishing spot. The subsequent explosion would shock and kill every living thing in the vicinity.

I'd like to go back someday to see if the few remaining upstream from Khone Falls have survived grenades and fishermen's nets.

MYANMAR

*Farmers moonlight during the dry season prospecting for gold along the banks of the Mekong. Most of the panners are women and children who yield a mere 100 baht ($4) per person per day for their efforts.*

BANVINAI

THAILAND

*Their world rapidly*
*changing around them,*
*a displaced Hmong hill tribe*
*family poses in traditional*
*dress against a backdrop of*
*Holland's Keukenhoff*
*Gardens at a photography*
*studio set up at the*
*Banvinai refugee camp*
*in Thailand.*

CHIANG SAEN • THAILAND

*To the accompaniment of horns and drums, amateur kickboxers go at it with feet, fists and elbows flying. Kickboxing is the main*

*form of entertainment during Chiang Saen's planting festival to mark the beginning of the dry season.*

CHIANG SAEN • THAILAND

*Disco dancing is the amusement of choice among the youth of Chiang Saen in Thailand's Golden Triangle,*

*where the Mekong forms the borders of Laos, Thailand and Myanmar (Burma).*

*A Hmong farmer prepares
his first bowl of opium for
the day before heading to the
fields in Kiew Kang in the
infamous Golden Triangle,
where most of the world's
opium is harvested.*

PAK CHOM

THAILAND

*A lone fisherman, viewed*
*from the shores of Pak Chom*
*in Thailand, maneuvers*
*his canoe through the shallows*
*of the Mekong beneath*
*the low-lying hills of Laos.*
*At the peak of the dry season,*
*the river will drop a total of*
*300 feet, exposing even more*
*rocks and sandbars, making*
*navigation often treacherous.*

65

LUANG PRABANG • LAOS

*A monk sweeps the courtyard of Wat Xieng Thong as part of his morning ritual of chores in Luang Prabang, the old royal capital of Laos.*

LUANG PRABANG • LAOS

*Young monks share a communal breakfast at Wat Xieng Thong, after their daily ritual of binthabat, or rice collecting, throughout town.*

*Every Lao male voluntarily trains as a monk for at least three months of his life.*

PAK LAY • LAOS

*Elephants like Toum, this 50-year-old female, outnumber cranes and bulldozers in Laotian logging operations along the Mekong.*

*Hardwood is Laos's second largest export, just behind hydroelectric power generated by Nam Ngum Dam on a tributary of the river.*

*preceding pages:*
VIENTIANE • LAOS

*The Mekong during the dry season is so shallow at Vientiane that people can practically wade across its entire width into Thailand.*

71

NAM NGUM • LAOS

*A former teak forest is reduced to skeletal branches piercing the surface of Nam Ngum Lake, formed by the damming of a Mekong tributary.*

*Underwater loggers still cut the valuable wood, most of it bound for sawmills in Thailand.*

KHONE FALLS

LAOS

*Two fishermen confront the
raging cataracts of Khone
Falls, gingerly tossing their
nets to catch fish as they
jump through the rapids
upstream. The falls, at the
Laos/Cambodia border,
thwarted the efforts of early
explorers searching for an
inland route to China.*

TONLE SAP • CAMBODIA

*Barrage-net fishermen pull a 300-pound carp from the Tonle Sap, north of Phnom Penh. The lake, Cambodia's richest fishing spot,*

*is also the Mekong's regulator, collecting the overflow from the river during the rainy season and swelling to five times its normal size.*

# Great Water

FROM THE NARROW CONFINES OF KHONE FALLS, THE Mekong broadens in Cambodia to lake-size proportions—two or three miles wide—as it sprawls along its way into the interior. Its name here, *Tonle Thom* (Great Water), could not be a more accurate description. Here the Mekong's flow is uncontrolled, regularly spilling over its banks, pouring its muddy waters into the river's regulator, the Tonle Sap—the Mekong's most important tributary. This is the only waterway in the world that actually changes its direction twice a year. During the wet season, June through October, excess water flows northward upriver into the Tonle Sap Lake, swelling it to five times its size. Come the dry season, November to May, the river reverses its flow, gradually draining the lake and thus naturally regulating the water that reaches the delta in the south, keeping it constantly supplied throughout the year.

Watching over this cycle of wet and dry at the northern end of the great lake is Angkor Wat, the monumental temple complex that was once the capital of the kingdom that ruled a large part of the Mekong River basin from the ninth to the thirteenth centuries. Abandoned, if not forgotten, Angkor has emerged from the past two decades marked by the war that raged around it and deteriorating due to water eroding its foundation and layers of jungle vegetation clinging to its facades. Since 1986, however, teams of archaelogists under United Nations auspices, with the help of hundreds of Khmer laborers, have been attempting to restore the monument to its former glory.

Angkor can be reached by ferry in two days or by air in two hours from Cambodia's present day capital of Phnom Penh, but I traveled there the hard way, overland by Jeep, along war-torn Route 5. On the map it looked simple enough—six inches of red line called the International Main Road circled the great lake, a distance of less than 200 miles. But the reality was three days of bone-jarring driving, over the most mud-holed, bomb-cratered obstacle course imaginable, best suited to the main local form of transportation, an ox cart.

We started the trip in high spirits, Men Saman, my government guide, Sok Dara, our driver, who had an international reputation among journalists and photographers who frequented the region as the best in Indochina, and I. Dara's specialty was sizing up the bomb-damaged, dilapidated bridges we frequently had to cross, rearranging single planks under the wheels (some narrower than the width of the tires) and driving straight and true over them as we admired his style from the safety of the roadside.

Our first breakdown happened the second day, just outside the town of Battambang, our destination for that evening. One too many potholes left us with a broken spring 20 miles shy of our stop for the night, with darkness approaching. A look at Men Saman's face told me the seriousness of our predicament. A survivor of Pol Pot's four-year (1975–79) reign of terror, Saman had witnessed the death of his entire family—parents and six children—and had been sent to a Khmer Rouge work camp not far from where we stood. The Khmer Rouge, led by Pol Pot, murdered or caused the death of one million people, about one-eighth of the population, in a misguided attempt to revolutionize the country with a forced return to an agrarian peasant culture.

Despite the fact that a peace accord had been signed in 1991, the Khmer Rouge remained armed, and sporadic raids were always a possibility. Saman explained, "the night still belongs to the Khmer Rouge." He instructed me in the use of an AK-47, pulled from its hiding place behind the front seat of the Jeep. "You just throw this lever down, point it and pull the trigger."

As if in answer to our silent wishes as we stood stranded by the roadside, two motorcycles made their way towards us. Obligingly, they took us to a small village a few miles down the road, where we spent the night in an orphanage. Listening to more tales of loss and tragedy far into the night and waking to see the faces of war in the abandoned children here brought the horror of the civil war's violence home to me.

I finally arrived at Angkor with great anticipation, breaking one of my golden rules—I always tell myself, as a professional traveler, that it is better not to have too many expectations about a place, otherwise you're bound to be disappointed. But I had dreamed of visiting Angkor since college days as an Asian history major, and this time I was definitely not disappointed.

I arrived before sunrise, with only the silhouette of the towers visible against the pink predawn sky. I stood alone, the spectacle of Angkor all to myself, and broke a second golden rule—when you see a picture, shoot it immediately, as there may be no second chance. There were pictures everywhere, the light was perfect, but I spent the next hour just wandering, listening to the sounds of my footsteps on ancient stone, savoring the private viewing.

There is a local saying, "The Lao live near the water, the Cambodians on it and the Vietnamese in it." As we progressed around the great lake, I found this to be true, at least the Cambodian and Vietnamese parts of it. At our first stop, Kampong Chnang, stilt houses as tall as three-story buildings loomed precariously over the shoreline. I climbed up and through this labyrinth of bamboo one evening in search of the perfect sunset, marveling at the local engineering skills. These lanky towers were built to withstand the 30-foot rise and fall of the great lake between wet and dry seasons. Should the waters rise more than 30 feet, as occasionally happens, the floors of the homes are moveable and are merely raised a few notches above the waterline.

But it is the indigenous Vietnamese here (easily identifiable by their conical straw hats) who have completely adapted to the aquatic lifestyle by living on the water in what look like floating towns made of houses and boats. As I sat on the veranda of a floating school in one such community near the shores of Siem Reap, I photographed an entire armada of lake life passing before me. There was the vegetable boat, the fruit boat, the noodle soup boat, the floating flower shop, the audio cassette boat. There were even floating pig farms, perched atop floating fish cages. Farmers fed the pigs, and the pigs, kept above the latticed cages, fed the fish with their droppings.

I stopped by the floating barbershop for a quick cut and some conversation. The barber explained, "as the lake waters recede, we move toward the deeper water in the middle, following the fish that live under us. At the lowest depth of the dry season, the fishing is easiest as the fish become more and more concentrated in less and less water. We then build a stilt house so the fish we catch can be set out to dry."

A year later, in far away America, I was to read about the fate of these peaceful fishermen. The Khmer Rouge, in a desperate attempt to disrupt the April 1992 elections—the first in 20 years—attacked this community, and killed more than a dozen ethnic Vietnamese, perhaps some of whom I had visited and photographed. Even for those living in the middle of the lake, far from the shores, there is no guarantee of safety in Cambodia.

*preceding pages:*  STUNG TRENG  •  CAMBODIA

*Clouds form an ominous canopy during the rainy season at Stung Treng.*

ROUTE ONE • CAMBODIA

*A house for two seasons: stilt houses weather the river's ups and downs during the wet and dry seasons. This home, outside Phnom Penh,*

*was photographed in February's drought (facing page) and October's floods (above).*

KIEN KLAENG

CAMBODIA

*A farmer takes advantage of the flood-swollen Mekong outside Phnom Penh to fill his irrigation buckets. The river broadens to three and a half miles here, making it possible for even ocean-going vessels to pass through.*

PREK PNEOU

CAMBODIA

*Each January, families from
up to 100 miles away travel to
the banks of the Tonle Sap,
north of Phnom Penh, during
prahak fishing season. They
buy their annual supply of
the tiny fish, to be salted and
prepared as a sauce, one of the
staples of the Cambodian diet.*

ANGKOR THOM • CAMBODIA

*One of the gargantuan faces on the towers of the Banyon casts an enigmatic gaze over the walls of the city.*

ANGKOR WAT • CAMBODIA

*Workers, reclaiming the great temple from the ravages of time and war, scour the front facade of Angkor Wat, as part of a United Nations restoration project begun in 1986.*

ANGKOR WAT

CAMBODIA

*From Angkor, the former
capital of the great kingdom
that ruled the entire
Mekong river basin between
the ninth and the thirteenth
centuries, only a handful of
the hundreds of stone
Buddhas that adorned the
temples have survived years
of war and looting.*

ANGKOR WAT • CAMBODIA

*The dancing Apsara, the mythological entertainers of Hindu gods, are one of the principal motifs in Khmer temple carvings.*

PHNOM PENH • CAMBODIA

*Reviving centuries-old traditions all but lost in the Khmer Rouge's campaign of terror, the School of Fine Arts in Phnom Penh trains a new generation of classical dancers.*

PHNOM PENH · CAMBODIA

*A poster artist puts the finishing touches on a likeness of Prince Sihanouk, celebrating his return*

*in 1992 from a thirteen-year exile prompted by the Khmer Rouge takeover.*

# The Four Faces

IN CAMBODIA THE MEKONG HAS ALWAYS BEEN THE DOMINANT geographic feature shaping the country's fortunes, running its length from north to south. And of all the towns and cities along it, the Cambodian capital of Phnom Penh, with a million people the largest city on the entire river, depends on it the most. The city is located at the *Chattomukh* (Four Faces), where the Mekong converges with the Tonle Sap river from the northeast and the Basak river flowing southwest, before branching off again to head south to the sea. I arrived in Phnom Penh on Prachem Ben, the Buddhist Day of the Dead.

Buddhism, all but wiped out by the Khmer Rouge, is now enjoying a revival, having been designated once again as the national religion. Men Saman, my official guide, explained the festival's meaning: "All the dead come to the pagodas on this day to find their relatives. If the family can't be found, they will be scolded by the spirits, and won't be successful in business." As every Cambodian has lost at least one relative at the hands of the Khmer Rouge, the streets were jammed with people.

With Phnom Penh's one traffic light out of service, hundreds of bicycles, *cyclos*—adult-sized passenger-carrying tricycles, Phnom Penh's primary source of public transportation —and motorcycles jammed the thoroughfare and made crossing the street a hazardous undertaking. I busied myself trying to break the photographic record for documenting the number of passengers on one *cyclo* (eight—including driver) and the number of people riding on a single motorcycle (six). Swept up in the crush of women in sarongs, laden with offerings of fish, fruit, chickens and sticky rice, I followed them

93

to the *wat*, where we ran the gauntlet of beggars lining both sides of the temple gates. The women gave generously—both food and money—as most of these unfortunates were amputees maimed by land mines.

Some 300 people a month continue to be crippled by explosions of the estimated 600,000 live mines scattered throughout the country, making this Cambodia's biggest health problem, ranking with malaria on the scale of physical hazards. In fact, not a day goes by in Cambodia without a reminder of the devastating effects of land mines. The limbless are everywhere, begging in front of hotels, restaurants, shops, wherever foreigners gather. Some put red dye on their wounds to heighten the grisly effect. Mines are a constant concern for anyone not walking on concrete or asphalt.

The land mine—"anti-personnel" as they are called—is one of humanity's cruelest inventions. It is made with just enough explosive charge to maim rather than kill, the idea being that it is more costly to the enemy army to rehabilitate a wounded soldier than to bury a dead one. Chinese, Russian and American mines of all types and sizes have been buried by both sides in the country's conflict, most often placed in areas frequented by civilians—around a wooded area where the locals need to gather firewood, for example, making it impossible for residents to avoid mine locations. And with each rainy season, the odds of stepping on a mine increase, for today's modern land mines are mostly made of plastic (the more difficult to find with metal-detecting minesweepers), which also means they can float. Thousands of these lethal charges have floated away with the floods, literally spreading out all over the countryside.

I visited the 1/79 hospital (named for the date on which the Vietnamese liberated Phnom Penh from the Khmer Rouge), the largest military hospital in the city, devoted solely to the treatment of land-mine victims. All 300 beds were filled, with many more patients spilling out into the hallways, forced to live on makeshift platforms, with only their wives, girlfriends or mothers to attend to them. These men, I learned, are actually the lucky ones. Though the hospital is understaffed, these patients are at least receiving care, however unsanitary the accommodations and scarce the medical supplies. I had to wonder about all those victims who never made it to the hospital, who bled to death in a paddy.

I could not afford to ask those questions. I shot quickly, methodically. To allow myself to think, to feel, would have made it impossible to shoot. There would be time for emotion later.

The dry season's windless heat was unbearable. Bundles of bloody bandages lay heaped on the floor. The buzzing sound of flies was everywhere. Yet the soldiers were astonishingly gracious in their suffering. They willingly described the circumstances in which they lost their limbs. At least somebody, I guess they thought, cared enough to want to know their story. Their hope was that word of their plight would somehow bring the help of foreign governments to Cambodia.

After leaving the hospital, I went to look for the brighter side of this sad story. Across the Mekong at Kien Klaeng, a privately funded group of American Vietnam war veterans run a prosthetics clinic and a vocational training center on an island smack in the middle of the river.

Ron Podlaski, a big blond-haired, red-faced All-American from Brooklyn, greeted me with a warm handshake. "We take only worst-case victims here—double amputees and the blind, those nobody else wants or can care for." Ron had just come back from Jaipur, India, with a plane-load of aluminum, rubber and plastic, and four Indian technicians. He passionately told me, "Our Jaipur limb is the best damned artificial limb out there—easy to make and fit, comfortable and cheap. We also make the best wheelchairs."

The group, he explained, was in the process of establishing a factory to mass-produce limbs and wheelchairs, first for the 53 families that lived here at the clinic and then for the thousands more in need. That is, if they could solve the problem of getting a constant supply of electricity, as well as a steady supply of raw materials. Their generator was down and the Mekong was up, making the delivery of supplies by boat difficult.

When I visited, the classrooms were in operation after a three-month search for teaching talent. Pol Pot, the leader of the Khmer Rouge, systematically killed most teachers when he drove the residents of Phnom Penh into forced labor camps in the countryside. Vocational classes here are designed to train the handicapped to eventually rejoin the work force. Housing is provided for them and their families in the meantime. Classes consist of the study of music for the blind, typing, draftsmanship and sewing for the amputees. English is offered for all.

The problems facing Ron Podlaski in trying to get the clinic and the prosthetics factory off the ground in the tiny community of Kien Klaeng were the same as those facing Phnom Penh and the nation trying to rebuild itself after the nightmare of 20 years of warfare. The optimism and enthusiasm for both tasks are unmistakable. Though the facades of the city look tired and worn, in need of new paint and plaster, the pure energy of its people, the out-and-out hustling, the traffic madness, the frenzied disco dancing, I took as positive signs that this city is ready to be on its way to recovery.

Phnom Penh's physical appearance owes much to the French, but its business ethic is essentially Chinese entrepreneurial. Capitalism is alive and well in Phnom Penh. I carried my money (at the time, 850 *riel* to the dollar) in a large L. L. Bean daypak strapped to my back to cope with rampant inflation. A beer war was raging between rival brands: Tiger, Anchor, Heineken and Carlsberg. Promotions and advertising for all four were plastered all over town. It seemed like a new restaurant or disco was opening every night to absorb dollars brought in by the ever-growing foreign aid community. Even marijuana, used as a spice in Cambodian soups, was being openly sold in the marketplace in quantities large enough to feed armies, perhaps to amuse the 20,000-strong UN peacekeeping forces newly arrived in town.

This $3 billion operation is the United Nations' largest. The commitment of troops has helped provide the under-pinnings of a tenuous truce. The return of Cambodia's former head of state, Prince Norodom Sihanouk, to Phnom Penh in November 1991, after more than 20 years in exile, was a symbolic high point in Cambodia's ongoing recovery. But the UN-sponsored elections of May 1993 did not herald in a new era of peace and prosperity so much as raise questions as to the Cambodians' ability to govern themselves democratically.

As I write this chapter, despite the mood of optimism coursing through Phnom Penh, the future of the country remains under a cloud of uncertainty. The Khmer Rouge remain a constant threat hovering just above the fragile coalition of feuding princes and parties that propose to carry Cambodia into the next decade. It remains to be seen whether the country can dispel the images of war, death and destruction that prompted the writer Colin Thubron to name Cambodia's Mekong "The River of Evil Memory."

PHNOM PENH • CAMBODIA

*Life has returned to this war-weary city, once emptied by Pol Pot, and a new generation decks itself in Sunday best for a moped cruise.*

*preceding pages:*

PHNOM PENH • CAMBODIA

*Cambodian flags, with the image of Angkor Wat emblazoned on them, are raised in tribute to mark the return of Prince Sihanouk.*

PHNOM PENH • CAMBODIA

*As Cambodia's economy struggles to revive itself, inflation is rampant. This sign painter*

*made 850,000 riel ($1,000) for installing a beer advertisement.*

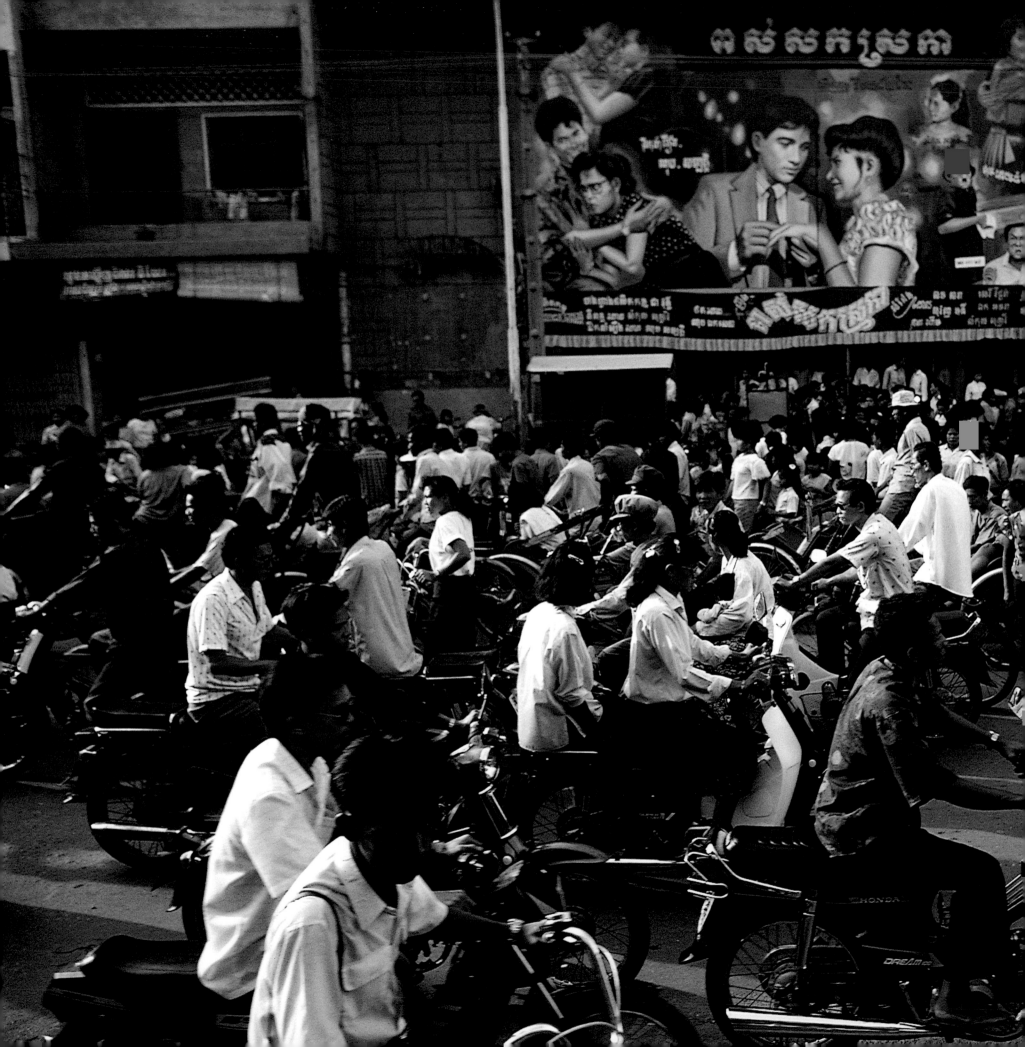

PHNOM PENH

CAMBODIA

*Phnom Penh on Sundays
teems with what seems
like its entire population
mingling in the crush
of wheels.*

PHNOM PENH

CAMBODIA

*Oarsmen compete in*
pirogue *races during the*
*Festival of the Turning of*
*the Waters. The festival*
*celebrates the reversal of the*
*flow of the Tonle Sap River*
*sending the waters of the*
*Tonle Sap Lake back into*
*the Mekong river after the*
*rainy season.*

ROUTE 5 • CAMBODIA

*The few temples that survived the destruction of the Khmer Rouge depend on donations for their upkeep. A larger-than-life monk extends a hand for alms on Route 5 outside Kampong Chnang.*

105

PHNOM PENH • CAMBODIA

*With the tentative new optimism in Cambodia, Buddhism is experiencing a resurgence. This factory is busy producing colorful Buddhas to replace the thousands destroyed by the Khmer Rouge.*

PHNOM PENH

CAMBODIA

*The first car of Cambodia's
only operating train is said
to be the the cheapest seat in
the country. Travel is free
for passengers who ride in
front on the run from
Battambang to Phnom
Penh because that car has
been specially weighted to
take the brunt of any
exploding mines the train
might encounter.*

PHNOM PENH

CAMBODIA

*Four victims of the*
*thousands of land mines*
*buried throughout*
*Cambodia pass the time at*
*the 1/79 Military Hospital*
*in Phnom Penh, named for*
*the date the Vietnamese*
*liberated the city.*

*A young mine victim at
the 1/79 Hospital, the
largest facility in the
country devoted entirely
to amputees, half of
whom are civilians.*

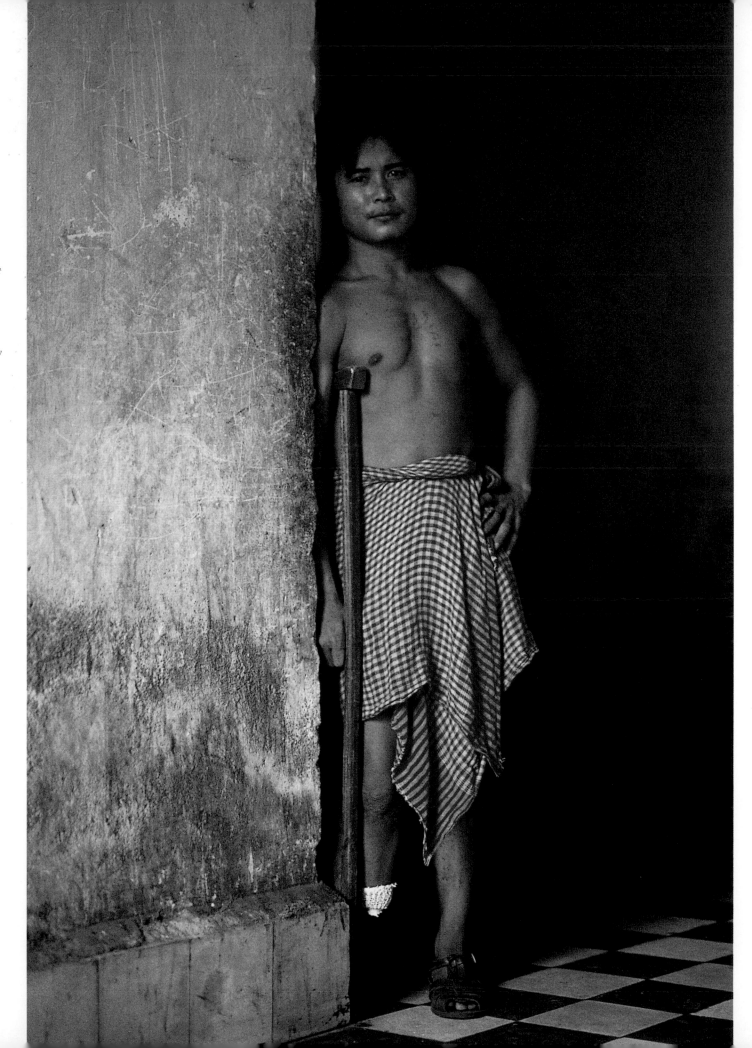

KAMPONG CHAM • CAMBODIA

*A shed at the edge of Kampong Cham's "killing field" holds hundreds of skulls heaped on the floor, a grim*

*reminder of the thousands who were killed and buried here in mass graves during the Khmer Rouge's reign.*

*Graffiti on the walls depict methods of killing children.*

NAM CAN • VIETNAM

*Defoliation during the war turned this mangrove forest at the mouth of the Mekong into a mud flat. At low tide, residents skim across the mud on boards,*

*searching for anything edible—cockles, crabs, octopus—to sell at markets as far away as Saigon.*

# River of Nine Dragons

THE VIETNAMESE CALL THEIR PART OF THE MEKONG *Cuu Long* (River of Nine Dragons) because the river divides into nine (in reality, eight, but ninc is believed to be a more auspicious number) branches as it spreads across the vast delta on its journey to the sea.

The Mekong Delta actually begins somewhere slightly south of Phnom Penh. We headed down Route 1, the main road, the only road between Phnom Penh and Saigon, Dara at the wheel of a brand-new Toyota Land Cruiser. It was early in the dry season. The now familiar, reassuring views of the mile-wide brown waters of the Mekong flanked us on the left-hand side of the road. My thoughts drifted back to college days, LIFE magazine–images of war and demonstrations and the draft. Some 20 years ago, at the height of the Vietnam War, a note

from a doctor kept me out of the army. And now I could not help but try to envision what it would have been like to be here as a soldier. It was casy to imagine the fear anyone would have felt, perhaps driving down this exact road en route to Saigon. River vistas, then closed-in jungle interspersed between small villages and rice paddies. Too many places to hide, to make ambushes, to set land mines. And as we drove deeper into the delta, the terrain became all the worse from a foot soldier's point of view, as dry land completely dissolved into wet, with boats out-numbering cars and canals replacing roads as the main arteries of transportation.

This is the character of the delta—one huge green swamp crisscrossed by an intricate maze of rivers, canals and irrigation ditches. Roads act as dikes, always the highest ground, connecting "islands" on which are built towns. I often ended the day with a stiff neck from the constant twisting and craning as I surveyed each side for a possible picture every time we passed over a bridge. I was rarely disappointed—intimate canal villages in the shadows on each side of the bank, crossed by rickety bamboo "monkey" bridges (so-called probably for the dexterity needed to traverse one) made for the typical scenery. Always there were boats, always people and everywhere water. I was like a proud father, proud that finally after all these miles of underutilized, untapped resource, I was now witnessing for the first time a huge population fully, joyously dependent on the waters from Tibet.

Vo Tung Xuon, a Harvard-trained agronomist who is known as "the Rice Doctor" in Vietnam, sums it up this way: "The Mekong is the elixir of life here. They do everything in it. Drinking, working, washing and farming in it. It's our most precious resource. It's too important to lose."

The delta is one of the world's great rice bowls, producing over half the country's rice crop (making Vietnam the third largest rice exporter in the world, behind Thailand and the US), supporting 15 million people, almost one-quarter of Southeast Asia's most densely populated country. The Mekong I'd come to know so well in so many incarnations was at last living up to its name, the Mother of Waters.

It was with some trepidation that I left Dara in Saigon and picked up Tran Van Viet, my new driver and government guide. Viet confided that he was a former Vietminh soldier who had fought against the French in Ben Trah, best known for its coconut plantations. He recounted how he and his fellow soldiers had lived up in the tops of trees, eating coconuts and picking off the enemy below. "When the Americans came to the delta, they lopped off the tops of our trees and sprayed chemical defoliants along our rivers and canals to take away our hiding places," he told me matter-of-factly.

The delta, especially the mangrove forest of U Minh (second in size only to the mangrove swamps of the Amazon basin), suffered the most extensive ecosystem damage of the war. Since the days of fighting the French, the delta had been the stronghold of the Vietcong, who chose the toughest, hottest, wettest and most mosquito-ridden environment in the country as their base of operations.

Today, though, few signs of war damage can be found anywhere. The mangrove forests were painstakingly replanted by the Vietnamese army. Mountains of war litter and scrap metal were dismantled, recycled or sold years ago. I found only a few things to photograph as evidence of the tumult of 20 years before: an occasional army helmet used as a water scoop, or a steel landing strip grate used as fencing.

The war has been recycled out of the Vietnamese mind as well. We were greeted almost everywhere with smiles and handshakes, and rarely was the war brought up as a topic of conversation. What seemed to be on everyone's mind was how to make a buck (literally, as the US dollar is the popularly accepted medium of exchange).

This obsession with making money is most obvious in the larger towns, where it was difficult to find rooms due to the large numbers of Asian businessmen working the delta like carpetbaggers. Our accommodations were usually rat-infested hovels called hotels, where rooms went for about $8 per night. (One late evening I suddenly awoke to discover a fat rat sitting on my stomach. I jumped, to its and my surprise, and it took off across the room, out from under the mosquito-netting, and disappeared into the dark.) The reception at these hotels was often overly friendly, with prostitutes banging on doors and windows into the early morning, begging, even demanding to be allowed in. A pair of earplugs my wife had left in my suitcase (she uses them as a defense against my snoring) became a welcome nightly necessity to shut out the sounds of urban life.

The surprisingly aggressive commercial side of the Vietnamese is perhaps best observed in Phung Hiep. There, at the confluence of seven canals, what is easily the world's biggest floating market congregates at sunrise, seven days a week. I hired a sculler, an ancient woman with a misshapen left foot caused by the constant pressure of the rhythmic pushing of her single oar, to take me into the midst of the market. She deftly navigated the crush of commerce as we jostled among hundreds of boats of all sizes and shapes, each carrying equally diverse cargoes of everything grown, picked, caught or manufactured in the delta.

The smaller boats scurried around larger ones with painted eyes; wholesalers displayed what they were buying on bamboo poles hung over the water. The haggling was dominated by women, the noise deafening. But for all the jockeying for position against the river's currents, never was a boat tipped or swamped, nor did I ever hear any shouts in anger. I was awed by how politely the boats passed each other, each respecting the other's space, the bigger ones taking care not to make any waves that would upset the smaller ones, whose gunnels were often only inches above the water.

Even as I was caught up by the excitement of Vietnam's focus on the future, the horror of the war that tore the country apart—in ways no overflowing river, no force of nature could—was brought back to me my last week in the country. On a tiny canal in the far southern town of Camau, I met the Monkey

Children. I had heard about them when a newspaper chronicled their plight a few years ago after they had been saved from a life as a featured attraction at a freak show in Saigon. Their name comes from their quick, animal-like movements, high-pitched squeaky voices and dwarfed bodies.

Their parents insist that the children's severe mental and physical deformities have been caused by the the chemical herbicide Agent Orange, which contains dioxin, known to cause birth defects. And according to Vietnamese officials, these children are but the tip of an iceberg of ongoing problems, ranging from an increase in miscarriages to an extremely high rate of infant mortality and congenital birth defects, all of which the government continues to document.

A FINAL IRONY OF THE DELTA'S REMARKABLE RECOVERY is the fact that once again the environment is under siege, the mangrove forests are again being destroyed, clear-cut to make way for shrimp farms financed by the Japanese hunger for five-inch tiger prawns. For centuries, the Mekong has retained its character as one of the wildest, least developed rivers in the world, but in less than 25 years it has hovered between possible destruction and rebirth as the lifeblood of Southeast Asia. The challenge to those who hope to sustain the river is to balance the voracious appetites of those drawn to its resources and the needs of those whose lives depend on it.

But after almost a year of following the river's currents, I'm certain that despite the assaults she's suffered and whatever lies ahead, this mother of all waters will continue her race from that holy mountain in Tibet to the South China Sea, nurturing the life along her banks for centuries to come.

PHUNG HIEP
VIETNAM

*Canals are the major*
*thoroughfares through the*
*densely populated Mekong*
*Delta, with boats of all*
*sizes cramming the*
*waterways en route to the*
*market in Phung Hiep.*

CHAU DOC

VIETNAM

*Fish farming is literally a*
*cottage industry along the*
*Mekong, with some 600*
*floating houses moored*
*near Chau Doc on the Vin*
*Te canal. Fish live under*
*the house in large cages*
*and are fed twice daily.*

PLAIN OF REEDS

VIETNAM

*Fishermen bring in their
haul with dip nets in the
Plain of Reeds, once a Viet
Cong stronghold and now
a new frontier for settlers
from overcrowded provinces
seeking land.*

*Flowers for the Tet New
Year celebrations fill the
market at Cantho, the
largest town in the Delta.*

123

VINH LONG • VIETNAM

*A merchant selling live birds takes advantage of captive customers in their idling cars waiting for one of the many ferries to carry them across the Delta's canals.*

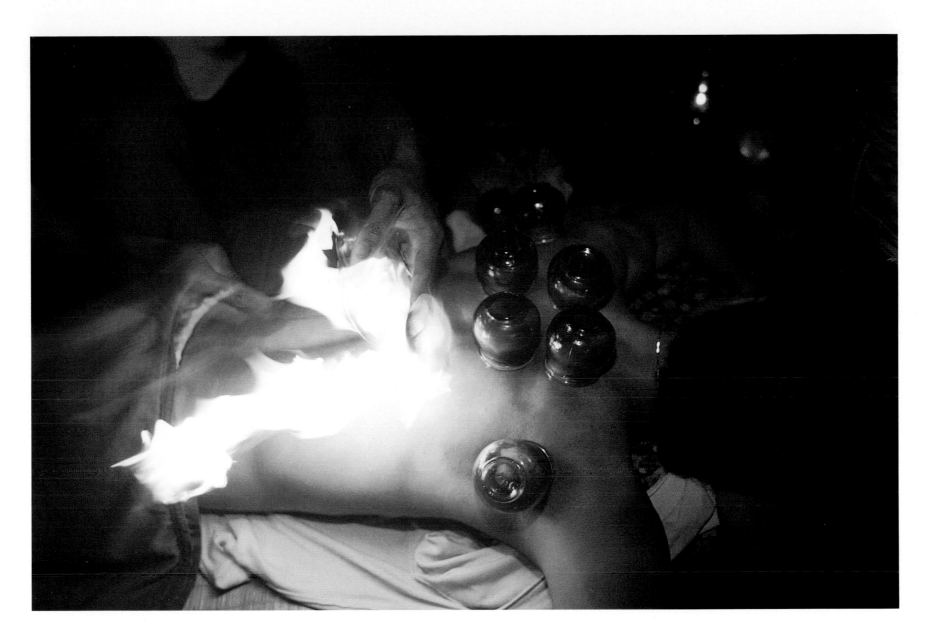

CANTHO • VIETNAM

*The ancient art of "cupping," the application of heated cups to the skin, is believed to release "bad air" and cure the body of a wide variety of ailments.*

SOC TRANG

VIETNAM

*At a rice mill in the heart
of Vietnam's "rice basket,"
women collect bran to sell
as animal feed. The factory
allows villagers, who also
use the husks for cooking
fires, to haul these waste
products away for free.*

127

VINH AN CANAL

VIETNAM

*Monkey bridges, so-called
because they require the
agility of a simian to
navigate, crisscross the
Delta, linking villages
and homesteads.*

CAMAU

VIETNAM

*A timeless scene along the*
*river: a woman silently*
*sculls en route to market.*

ACKNOWLEDGEMENTS

I would like to thank the following people who helped make this project possible: at the *National Geographic*, editor Bill Graves, director of photography Tom Kennedy and assistant director of photography Kent Kobersteen for their generous support; Seiichi Hasumi, president of Takarajima Books, and New York editors Akihiko Miyanaga and Kiyotaka Yaguchi; Bob Madden, for his enthusiasm; Bill Marr, for designing this book; Declan Haun, for his production work; Cathy Buchanan for her research assistance; Susan Bell, Joanne Camas and Elizabeth Bibb for editing; my China guide, Wen Dong, for getting me through many tight spots, often at great personal risk; Bill Herod of the Indochina Project and the Mekong Committee in Bangkok for securing the permission for our travel in Laos, Cambodia and Vietnam; Robert Kirschenbaum and Suzanne Goldstein of Pacific Press Service; Stanley Karnow for his insights into Indochina; John Hoskin and Allen Hopkins in Bangkok and Greg Davis in Tokyo for their good advice; my guides, Somnuk Chanthaseth in Laos; Bhanu Maneevathanakul in Thailand; Men Saman, Touch Seang Tana and Chhay Song Heng in Cambodia; Tran Van Viet and Vo Tong Xuan, "the Rice Doctor," in Vietnam; and finally, to my traveling companions, *National Geographic* picture editor Susan Welchman and writer Tom O'Neill, who also coached me in this, my first endeavor as a writer.

—Michael Yamashita

January, 1995